CHRISTMAS
That We Might Have *Life*

Twelve Reflections on the First Christmas through a Pro-Life Lens

Rev. Jim Harden, M.Div.

Christmas - That We Might Have Life
Twelve Reflections on the First Christmas through a Pro-Life Lens

By Rev. Jim Harden, M.Div.
© 2023 by Rev. Jim Harden, M.Div.
V2

All rights reserved. No part of this publication may be reproduced, stored in a retrieval system, or transmitted, in any form or by any means, electronic, mechanical, photocopying, recording, or otherwise, without prior written permission of the publisher. Printed in the United States of America.

Print Book ISBN: 979-8-9894922-2-0
An imprint of CompassCare.

Scripture quotations taken from the (NASB®) New American Standard Bible®, Copyright © 1977, by The Lockman Foundation. Used by permission. All rights reserved. Lockman.org.

For more information about CompassCare, go to *CompassCareCommunity.com*

An imprint from CompassCare
2024 W. Henrietta Rd. #6D
Rochester, NY 14623

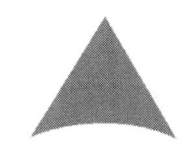

*An insightful Bible study
for your church or small group.*

Endorsements of Rev. Jim Harden, M.Div.

"Quite frankly... it's because of men and women like you [Rev. Harden] that we're at this moment where [Roe and Casey are] overturned."

Tony Perkins
The Washington Watch

"Thank God for what you're doing—and you're still doing it... We're all grateful for that."

Gov. Mike Huckabee
The Huckabee Show

"What you're doing is honorable. What you're doing is obviously your calling in life. And I admire you for it. I admire all the people who donate to you."

Sean Hannity
Fox News

"I just want to let you know; we have your back. 100%."

Charlie Kirk
Turning Point USA

"In times like these, there are always a handful of people who refuse to shut up and sit down. They change the world. Bonhoeffer, King and today the names include Jim Harden and those at CompassCare who refuse to bow down."

Glenn Beck
The Glenn Beck Program

"You are one of those heroes out there... It would be an amazing thing if instead of three CompassCare centers in the State of New York, there were 10—or 50!"

Eric Metaxas
The Eric Metaxas Show

"The minute Rev. Jim Harden walked on stage to film with Daystar, I was touched by his sincerity and wisdom. I am encouraged there are people like him to fight on behalf of the unborn: brave, forceful, and obedient to God."

Joni Lamb
Daystar Television Network

CHRISTMAS – THAT WE MIGHT HAVE LIFE

TABLE OF CONTENTS

Introduction 1

Devotion 1: Lessons from Baby Jesus 3

Devotion 2: Mother Mary and Her Unplanned Pregnancy 9

Devotion 3: The Gift of Christmas, the Power of Sacrifice 13

Devotion 4: Jesus, Shepherds, and the Political Elite 19

Devotion 5: Christmas and the Hidden Power of a Life Well Lived 23

Devotion 6: Unplanned Pregnancy Points to Christmas 30

Devotion 7: The Purpose of Christmas 37

Devotion 8: Mary and Elizabeth, The Power of Motherhood on Display 43

Devotion 9: Simeon, The Savior Stirring Hope 49

Devotion 10: Jesus' Plans Lighting the Way to Peace 55

Devotion 11: Wisemen, Heroes and God's Eternal Kingdom 61

Devotion 12: Christmas Is an Invasion? 67

Conclusion 73

About the Author 75

Introduction

Christmas is a time of vision, a time to consider the landscape of human life, what it means, and why it's valuable. The mental image of Christmas is the nativity, the crude circumstances that surrounded the moment when God reinforced the dignity of humanity by clothing Himself as one. But He did not stop there. For the joy set before Him, He invaded the dungeon of our sin-dimmed world with the light of His presence, to transfer us into His kingdom of light. He took on the life of a man that He might lay it down for us all, underscoring the value He places on each one of us. If sinless Jesus, God in the flesh, is invaluable, what does it say of the value He places on us if He exchanged His life for ours, becoming sin that He might destroy death? It is His resurrection that has the last, everlasting word: Christmas. The beginning of the end of sin and death. Christmas helps us see who God is and who we are. Christmas brings into focus the only two things that are sacred in this world—God and people. Christmas is about life. The Author of life. Your life. My life. And the life of the world.

It is my prayer that God will reveal Himself to you in deeper ways through these short pro-life Christmas reflections.

2

Devotion 1

Lessons from Baby Jesus

Baby Jesus came from heaven to earth to reflect what kind of person populates God's kingdom—a baby. Or said differently… helpless humans in need of a Redeemer.

Baby Jesus is the revelation that the all-powerful God of the universe is big enough to be humble.

Baby Jesus is the certainty that the vast storehouses of heaven were emptied for that which God treasures most—human beings.

Baby Jesus is the encouragement that trial and hardship are not meant to be avoided but joyfully endured for the sake of others.

Baby Jesus is the reminder that real faithfulness is always tangible.

Baby Jesus was born to defeat sin and its consequence, death.

Baby Jesus came to demonstrate His victory over death by rising from the grave.

Baby Jesus was born to commission soldier souls to liberate those oppressed by sin and to protect others oppressed by sinners.

Baby Jesus was destined to say, "Permit the children to come to Me; do not hinder them; for the kingdom of God belongs to such as these. Truly I say to you, whoever does not receive the kingdom of God like a child will not enter it at all" (Mark 10:14-15).

Baby Jesus was born to reveal the litmus test of a true follower of God: "Whoever receives one child like this in My name receives Me; and whoever receives Me does not receive Me, but Him who sent Me" (Mark 9:37).

Dietrich Bonhoeffer said, "The test of the morality of a society is what it does for its children." It is no coincidence that the God of the universe revealed Himself in the form of a baby. He did not have to, but He did. Like God, we too must be open to loving and redeeming more human beings no matter what their age, socio-economic status, who their mother and father are, their health prognosis, their gender, or their perceived quality of life. For the world to reject a child, or to even consider rejecting a child, reveals a cold-heartedness echoing in the void of a self-indulgent way of life.

Baby Jesus was born so that we all, with one voice, would rejoice in the hope that life brings instead of mourning over what could have been, like "Rachel weeping for her children" (Matthew 2:18) killed by a Herod-like culture. In God, there is always room for one more light in this dark and lowly manger world.

> *In God, there is always room for one more light in this dark and lowly manger world.*

Questions for Reflection

Jesus came to earth as a baby. Why is that important?

_____

_____

_____

_____

_____

What does it mean that Jesus is the "Light of the World" and that we are to be a reflection of that Light?

_____

_____

_____

_____

_____

What message would God have you tell others about Baby Jesus?

_____

_____

_____

_____

_____

Father God,

Thank you for giving us your Son, Jesus, and bringing Him into this world as a baby. Teach us to be like a child, truly dependent on you, Father, always trusting in your love for us. We are thankful Jesus came to give us victory over death. We need you, God, our Redeemer.

Amen.

Devotion 2

Mother Mary and Her Unplanned Pregnancy

She did not plan on being pregnant. She was not even married. She was frightened. Her fiancé was going to end the relationship. Her community would disparage her and stigmatize the child. Feeling alone, she went away, to a place where she would be loved and insulated from the pressure and where she could ponder what this pregnancy might mean for her, the child, her community, and her world (Luke 1:39-56). Then, the government, having legalized infant killing, wanted the child dead.

Her name was Mary. Her fiancé's name was Joseph. And her child's name is Jesus. It is no coincidence that the circumstances giving rise to the world's greatest sin of our time, abortion, are precisely the same circumstances that gave rise to the only One who could save the world from sin.

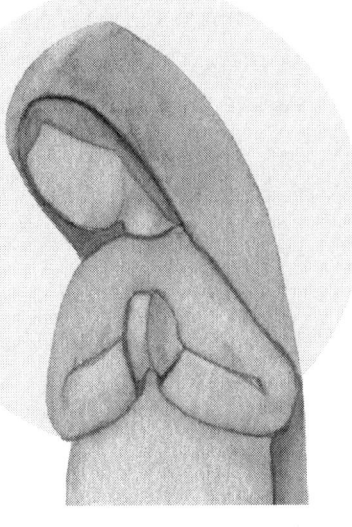

The Nativity story represents the story of each and every one of us. We, sinners, were powerless before a holy God. A sinful world conspired against our ability to have a flourishing life together with Him and our family. But the Lord intervened in a way that covered our sin and protected our lives from being destroyed. The cross allows us to be adopted as children of God. Our adopted status has given us access to God's throne, with full standing and a voice and power to leverage, like Christ, on behalf of the most vulnerable.

As it was for Mary, most pregnancies are a surprise. And welcome or not, each pregnancy represents the Lord's kind providence and intention for the parent to participate in His adorning of history with that new person. To a woman who is alone, an unplanned pregnancy can appear hopeless. But from God's view, there is no such thing as an unplanned pregnancy. And where there is life, there is hope.

Christmas reminds us that there is nothing sacred in this world but God and people. During the Christmas season, we remember the sacrifice God made by humbling Himself, becoming a man, and submitting Himself to the ignoble death on a cross. He drank the full cup of God's wrath against sin at the cross. He endured all this for the joy set before Him (Heb. 12:2) – the salvation of humanity from sin and death. Jesus' infinite sacrifice demonstrates the supreme worth our wise and holy Lord places upon people; people whom He calls His children (John 1:12-13).

Questions for Reflection

Thinking about the culture of the Ancient Days, what would you have done if you faced an unplanned pregnancy?

_____

_____

_____

_____

_____

How is that different than what women experience today?

_____

_____

_____

_____

_____

"Joy to the World" is an oft-sung Christmas carol. What does 'for the joy set before Him, Jesus endured the cross" mean?

_____

_____

_____

_____

_____

Father God,

As we ponder the many miracles surrounding Jesus' birth and the circumstances of Mary's pregnancy, we can't imagine both the amount of joy and the undeserved scorn she might have felt. One miracle we overlook is Mary's endurance and perseverance. May we look to her example when we are faced with challenges in life. May we always trust in your perfect plan for us.

Amen.

Devotion 3

The Gift of Christmas, the Power of Sacrifice

G.K. Chesterton once said something like, "God forbid the day ever comes when men do not commit murder simply because it is against the law."

The King of Righteousness, the King of Peace, is celebrated as coming in the flesh during the Christmas season. The purpose of that coming was to enact a 'better covenant' (Hebrews 8:6) where the actions of people were not constrained by the outside force of law, which is in perpetual conflict with a person's nature, which is to live purely for themselves. Rather, that new deal between God and man made possible through the revelation of the indestructible life of Jesus celebrated at Christmas, causes the law of the life of God to become our new nature. Indeed, it causes our good and right actions to be in true integrity with who we really are in Christ.

When we live according to this new deal, this 'better covenant,' we don't do wrong because we intuitively know certain things are simply morally wrong… like abortion. We know this because those who follow Christ have willfully laid down what they hold most dear, like so much gold, frankincense, and myrrh; their very selves, their old nature, placing it at the feet of Christ in exchange for His nature, reflecting His desires, freely.

And so, it is only natural that those dedicated to Christ live in an upright fashion, freely, effortlessly acting out the desire of God to exercise mercy and justice, to act toward others as He presently acts toward those who seek Him.

To be clear, being upright and acting upright can be two very different things. Being upright means you are free to act in accordance with who you really are and reflect the nature of God. Acting upright simply means you try really, really hard to be good as you perceive it. The first is done in the power of God, and the second is done in our own power. The first lasts forever because our actions naturally come from the indestructible, indescribable eternal life of Jesus, while the second is lost and forgotten because it issues from something less.

The freedom we have in Christ allows us to be free from care related to material wealth so that we are free to use our actions for the sake of mercy and justice. By God's grace and strength, we leverage our worldly goods, including what power and influence we have, on behalf of those women and babies who so desperately need it, even when it calls for the personal sacrifice of time, talents, and treasure.

In the spirit of the wise men, the Christmas season is an appropriate time for ***generous gifts*** as an act of reflection on the power God has given you through Christ to freely change the world. "For where your treasure is, there your heart will be also." (Luke 12:34)

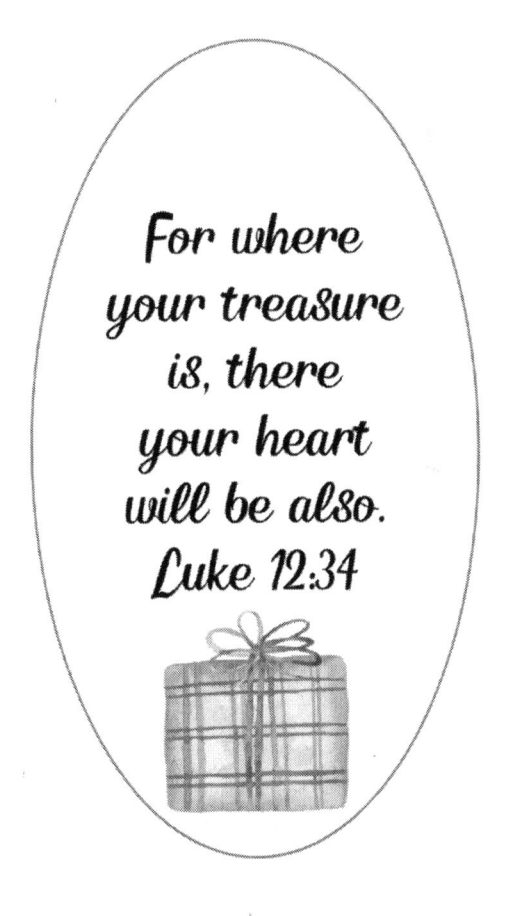

> *For where your treasure is, there your heart will be also.*
> *Luke 12:34*

Questions for Reflection

What is the difference between acting good under our own power vs. a life dedicated to Christ, reflecting the nature of God in our actions?

_____

_____

_____

_____

_____

The "New Covenant" reference in Hebrews 8 concludes with the phrase, "For I will be merciful toward their wrongdoings, and their sins I will no longer remember." (Hebrews 8:12). Why is this significant in light of the Nativity?

_____

_____

_____

_____

_____

The wise men gave gifts to Jesus. Years later, Jesus spoke these words in Luke 12:34: "For where your treasure is, there your heart will also be." What is one way you might connect these two ideas together this Christmas?

_____

_____

_____

_____

_____

Lord God,

Thank you for the gift of Christmas. Thank you for the life we have because of Jesus. Let us honor His sacrifice and gift of eternal life through our own sacrifices of time, talent, and treasure gifts to others during this season.

Amen.

Devotion 4

Jesus, Shepherds, and the Political Elite

What were the times like that first Christmas? Certainly, the first public proclamation of Jesus' birth by the angel to the lowly shepherds was a sign of 'good news and great joy for all the people' (Luke 2: 10). It is no coincidence that lowly shepherds were given the honor as the first recipients of the royal proclamation representing the poor, the weak, the marginalized, those out in the proverbial cold and dark of society. It is no coincidence that the worldly powerful had to blindly grope for any morsel of news about this atomic bomb of history. And to the shepherds, this Jesus born in solidarity with them revealed a glimpse into the resplendent glory of the heaven awaiting. Thousands of angels voiced praise to the Most High, now wrapped in rags. It was cause for rejoicing, for the Savior's birth was 'for them' (Luke 2:11), those with rags for armor and pain for comfort.

But there was treachery and scheming going on. A lurking and real danger moved in the shadows. For the hard work of redeeming a lost people—the blind, deaf, crippled, possessed, poor and wretched—is a war. It is a fight for the dignity and liberation of each person, yes, for exploited pregnant women and their dehumanized babies. This work, while pure joy for those saved, is vile to the politically powerful and met with vitriol.

"Then an angel of the Lord appeared to Joseph in a dream and said, 'Get up! Take the Child and His mother and flee to Egypt, and remain there until I tell you; for Herod is going to search for the Child to destroy Him'" (Matthew 2: 13). Herod, realizing that the magi who were supposed to report back had tricked him, ordered the killing of all male children two years old and younger within the vicinity of Bethlehem (Matthew 2: 12, 16-18).

The book of Revelation clarifies what was really happening with Herod and the nativity, "And the dragon stood before the woman who was about to give birth so that when she gave birth he might devour the child" (Rev 12:4b).

The following days, those between Jesus' birth and His second coming, those times in which you and I now live, are described like this, "And there was war in heaven . . . And they [the believers] overcame him [the great dragon] because of the blood of the lamb [Jesus' death on the cross] and because of the word of their testimony [how Jesus had freed them from bondage to sin], and they did not love their life even when faced with death" (Revelation 12: 7a, 11).

Christmas is a war and the war rages on. The nativity is a battleground for every life.

It is a battle for the soul; the restoration of each human to God is what the cross is all about. And the call of the believer is no different. We are called to the same self-sacrifice on behalf of others, loving God and others more than even our own life. As the Apostle Peter says, "For you have been called for this purpose, since Christ also suffered for you, leaving you an example for you to follow in His steps" (I Peter 2: 21). The salvation of others depends on our ability to follow Christ so well, to be so much like heaven as to be unrecognizable by a fallen world, to be so enamored with the glory of God that we consider our suffering in this life as joy in comparison.

Christians are uniquely suited to know who those in bondage are because we also were in bondage. Christians are uniquely suited to understand the plight of the poor and powerless because we too were once poor and found true wealth. And now, so armed with this heavenly virtue of forgiveness and sacrifice found in Christ, the Christian ventures back into the bowels of this cavernous world to face the evil and free its slaves because that is what the King has done for him.

A woman is at risk for abortion because she is a casualty of war, oppressed by a twisted culture, offering death as a solution. A culture bent in on itself, unable to offer hope and real help. She is coerced, pressured to make a decision alone, pursued by fear . . . and the life of her baby hangs in the balance. Our joy is to set her free, to help her insulate her baby from the elements of this stormy world. This is Christmas; hers and ours, the morning star on the edge of night. These are the circumstances for joy, the circumstances that define generosity and the gospel of life.

Questions for Reflection

How would you describe the 'battle for our souls'?

___

___

___

___

___

What is the best way to fight that battle daily?

___

___

___

___

___

As a 'lowly shepherd' but with the power of the conquering King of kings inside us, one of the best ways to defeat the enemy is to share our testimony. Who will you share His truths with today?

_____

_____

_____

_____

_____

God, You have sent Jesus our conquering King. Thank you. Give us the boldness and strength to share our story of how you have saved us from death with others today. May we experience your joy as we embrace this battle today.

Because of the power of His name, Jesus.

Amen.

Devotion 5

Christmas and the Hidden Power of a Life Well Lived

"You call this a happy family! Why do we have to have all of these kids?" George Bailey exclaims to his wife while experiencing financial despair in the classic film *It's a Wonderful Life*. George's presumption: Children are a (financial) burden. You know the story. George soon learns that life is not about acquiring what the world has to offer. It's not about securing the world's education. It's not about seeing the world or even conquering the world. In the climax of the film on Christmas Eve, George never gets the high-paying job with the fancy clothes and travel opportunities. He never gets to go to school or even leave Bedford Falls. What George gets is a revelation from God. A revelation about how living and providing for others is inestimably more powerful than living and spending for oneself. In one scene there is a picture of George's father hanging on the wall at the Bailey Building and Loan office, the one institution standing between the people of Bedford Falls, and a devious, power-hungry banker named Potter. Under the picture it reads,

"The only thing you can take to heaven is what you give to others." Perhaps an echo of what Jesus says in Matthew 6:20: "But store up for yourselves treasures in heaven, where neither moth nor rust destroys, and where thieves do not break in or steal."

What Potter did, that "warped, frustrated, old man," was take advantage of people's unfortunate circumstances. What the Building and Loan did was provide the people with the freedom to become who they were meant to be. George's father was the founder of the Building and Loan and when he died Potter made a motion that the board of directors dissolve the company, leaving the population of Bedford Falls at the mercy of Potter's evil schemes. Seeing the future injustice and abuse, George addressed the board saying, "This town needs this measly one-horse institution if only to keep people from having to go crawling to Potter."

Maybe the multi-billion-dollar international abortion industry is like Potter conspiring to take advantage of women facing unplanned pregnancy. And maybe pro-life Christians are like the little Bailey Building and Loan working vigorously to offer the gift of vision to a woman drowning in a river of overwhelming circumstances, a vision of her future after having a baby. Without pro-life people working through pregnancy centers, most of the women at risk for abortion would be forced to go with the only alternative available to them and make the tragic choice of terminating their pregnancy.

Not a sane woman alive wants to have an abortion. Women seriously considering abortion do so because they feel stuck, like they have no choice; they feel like they *need* an abortion. Pro-life Christians, acting through organizations like pregnancy centers, like the Bailey Building and Loan, stand in the gap and champion the cause of those in desperate need of alternatives to twisted agendas and unethical practices.

Like George, the extent of your life's positive impact on others may not be obvious to you now. But be assured that if you help even one woman to have her baby, it will have eternal significance.

The only thing you can take to heaven is what you give to others.

Questions for Reflection

Because of your faith in Jesus, have you ever 'stood up for the little guy' or made a decision that seemed to go against the norm?

_____

_____

_____

_____

_____

How can you invest in eternal treasures in heaven while you are alive on earth?

_____

_____

_____

_____

_____

What are some tangible ways to combat injustice?

_____

_____

_____

_____

_____

Father God,

Thank you for Jesus. He bridged the gap between a world that wants to defeat us and your eternal plan for an eternal relationship with us. Give us eyes to see injustices in the world and the courage to stand up for them. Help us invest in heavenly treasures today.

Amen.

Devotion 6

Unplanned Pregnancy Points to Christmas

A woman facing unplanned pregnancy is a Christmas metaphor. Not Mary's unexpected pregnancy with Jesus, but Israel's need for a savior—stuck, lost, mired in a series of faithless decisions resulting in the loss of physical and moral freedom. Like Israel, she is unable to resolve the crisis without powerful intervention from the outside. A woman considering abortion is shipwrecked on the same reef of despair as you and I were, and as the nation of Israel was before Christ's birth.

The stormy elements of unplanned pregnancy drive a woman to think abortion is her lifeboat, not because she feels empowered by "choice" but because her circumstances bully her into it. When a woman facing an unplanned pregnancy comes to a pregnancy center like CompassCare, she says in so many words that she is trapped and that abortion is her only option. She is often in anguish and feels powerless, having lost what she desired for her life. Much like 'Rachel weeping for her children' (Jeremiah 31:15; Matthew 2:18), the only way to dry her tears is to realize the hope that has been made apparent through Christ's birth. Israel was stripped of her inheritance under God's judgment and deported to Babylon for her sin. Yet, God had a plan to deliver her through the incarnation of His Son, called Immanuel, which translated means "God with us" (Matthew 1:23). The arrival of Jesus signaled the final end to the cause of their weeping which the LORD, through Jeremiah, commanded saying, "Restrain your voice from weeping and your eyes from tears" (Jeremiah 31:16) for "He will save His people from their sins" (Matthew 1:21).

But how will this salvation happen? The Savior's work would fulfill the covenant of law under Moses when God freed the people from their bonds in Egypt (Matthew 2:15; Jeremiah 31:32). After all, Jesus says in Matthew 5:17, "Do not think I came to abolish the Law or the Prophets; I did not come to abolish but to fulfill." Jeremiah says, "'Behold, days are coming,' declares the LORD, 'when I will make a new covenant with the house of Israel and with the house of Judah… for they will all know Me, from the least of them to the greatest of them,' declares the LORD, 'for I will forgive their iniquity, and their sin I will remember no more'" (Jeremiah 31:31, 34). This is God's plan of redemption. This is the glorious reality of His grace, worked out among sinners. The nativity is the dawning of the long-awaited morning star of restoration rising over Israel's perpetual night as God "became flesh and dwelt among us" (John 1:14) and was revealed to all—the small (lowly shepherds, Luke 2:8ff) and the great (King Herod, Matthew 2:3). And His work on the cross, the very purpose for His coming, the new covenant in Christ's blood, has the power to free us from our bondage under sin when we submit to Him, rather than continue to be ruled by our passions. God has given pro-life Christians the ability to offer these women that same assurance of peace through salvation that comes only from Jesus.

Make no mistake. A woman facing an unplanned pregnancy is not considering abortion simply because of financial pressure, an apathetic father, or educational inequality, but rather, because of the darkness of a world ruled by the great yet merciless Herodian-like grip of sin. The trespass of abortion today is not an escape hatch from the consequence of yesterday's sin. There is only one way of escape.

Because Jesus came through a manger and bore the burden of our sin on the cross, we are now free in the power of the Holy Spirit to "Bear one another's burdens, and thereby fulfill the law of Christ" (Galatians 6:2). Pro-life Christians through pregnancy centers like CompassCare serve women seriously considering abortion by offering the treasure of truth about who they are as humans made in the image of God and their need for restoration with Him. In the process, we can dignify her by truly caring enough to empower her with the ethical medical care and community support she needs to have her baby.

Together with Jeremiah we can say to her and to each other, "'There is hope for your future,' declares the LORD, 'And your children will return to their own territory'" (Jeremiah

31:17). Our territory as humans is walking with God. "What then shall we say to these things? If God is for us, who can be against us?" (Romans 8:31).

Questions for Reflection

Describe the parallels between a woman facing an unplanned pregnancy and our own need for a Savior.

_____

_____

_____

_____

_____

How is the manger similar to a pro-life pregnancy center?

_____

_____

_____

_____

_____

What is our role in the decision of a woman facing an unplanned pregnancy?

_____

_____

_____

_____

_____

Father God,

Thank you for the illustration of the woman facing an unplanned pregnancy and how it points to our own need for a Savior. Everything you create, you have a plan to redeem. And you have provided reconciliation through the manger in Bethlehem to the cross of Calvary. It is only Through Jesus that we have life. We are grateful.

Amen.

Devotion 7

The Purpose of Christmas

What is the purpose of Christmas? Certainly, Jesus the Christ, our Savior, is born. But why do we humans need a savior? And why does it have to be Jesus?

Why does humanity need a Savior? Because we have fallen from grace. God created the first man Adam, upright and good. As the head of all mankind, Adam's actions were imbedded in all humans that followed. The first man's primary decision that impacted you and me was to deliberately disobey God's one and only express command. Due to Adam's sin, mankind now has a natural bent to step away from his created destiny, reflecting God's glory, in order to turn inward and please ourselves alone. Since sin removes us from the source of all life, God, death reigns over all the earth. As the old Christmas hymn 'O Holy Night' goes, "Long lay the world in sin and error pining...."

Everyone dies. Mankind needs to be saved from our spiritual condemnation and physical death caused by sin. But why does our Savior have to be Jesus? In order to solve our sin and death problem we need a new nature, one that is righteous, which we cannot provide for ourselves. We need a new heart, to be recreated from the inside out. This recreation requires the power of the One who created (Hebrews 1:2) and sustains (Colossians 1:17-18) the world and humanity with His very word (John 1:1-5).

And one holy night over 2000 years ago, it was revealed that the "Word became flesh, and dwelt among us" (John 1:14a), with the precise purpose of recreating humanity and reconciling us with Himself, that we might live again. This meant that Jesus, God in the flesh, needed to become the new Adam, a second fountainhead for a renewed humanity. His act of obedience, death on a cross (Philippians 2:8) in our place, would defeat the power of Adam's original act of sin which resulted in death (Romans 5:19). Jesus' death allows those who repent and submit to God to be acquitted from the judgment of spiritual condemnation (Romans 5:17) and opt into a new creation (2 Peter 3:13; Revelation 21:1). This is the gift given by God to humanity, renewed hope of life everlasting.

Christmas represents every person's only hope all year long. Jesus has come to save us from our sin and its effects forever. So as women face unplanned pregnancy, hopeless and haunted by the prospect of the death of her planned life the world says she deserves, a life lived by herself and for herself, CompassCare and other pro-life pregnancy centers hover like the star over Bethlehem signifying the hope of Christmas to all women in crisis. Life for a woman considering abortion isn't over, it is just beginning. She finds herself facing an unplanned pregnancy, often because of a series of poor decisions. Salvation is not found in more of the same but in more of God. She says, "I'm stuck. My life as I planned it or want it is over." The pro-life pregnancy center nurse gives her the priceless gift of a vision of a hopeful and bright future for both her and her baby. She can be saved, and her baby too, not just physically but spiritually, since Christ is born and "died for our sins... and that He was raised on the third day" (1 Corinthians 15:3-5). Our God is powerful enough to care for and save each person's whole self and has promised to meet all our needs as a good father. He never promised an easy life. But He did promise us abundant life, as God defines abundant, if we submit to Him and sacrificially love our neighbor.

Extend the meaning of Christmas to pensive women contemplating death as a solution. For as the hymn 'O Holy Night' continues, "A thrill of hope the weary world rejoices, for yonder breaks a new and glorious morn." Let us continue together, with thankfulness, in awe, to invite the world to join us in fallen man's only appropriate response to a Savior so strong— "Fall on your knees."

*This is
the gift given
by God to
humanity,
renewed hope
of life
everlasting.*

Questions for Reflection

Everyone dies. Both a physical death and a spiritual death. Jesus came to give us life. But why do we need a savior?

_____

_____

_____

_____

_____

And why must that savior be Jesus?

_____

_____

_____

_____

_____

How can we bring life to women contemplating death this Christmas season?

_____

_____

_____

_____

_____

Father God,

Thank you for life. Life through newborn babies and life through Jesus. Give us the courage and strength to submit to you and love our neighbors so that we might find the promised abundant life. Thank you for hope. Thank you for Jesus, our Savior.

Amen.

Devotion 8

Mary and Elizabeth, The Power of Motherhood on Display

Who has more influence over humanity's prospects than a parent? Consider the maternal profession: who can hope to equal a mother's power over posterity? No teacher, coach, counselor, friend, politician, or program could ever compare to a mom by any measure. Certainly, no child denies his mother's monumental station in his life. And her significance extends beyond that. Her influence draws into the present grand echoes of ancient tradition, emblazoning them indelibly upon the far reaches of the future. Her career is linked with the sovereign hand of God, partnering to carry providence into the world one life at a time.

The Biblical nativity story demonstrates God's pleasure in a willing mother's generational impact writ large as two women submit to giving birth to two boys who will reorient fallen creation back to God.

Elizabeth viewed her barrenness as a disgrace, which God in His mercy cured shortly after the angel told her husband she would give birth to John the Baptist. So, Elizabeth says of herself, "This is the way the LORD has dealt with me... to take away my disgrace among men" (Lk 1:25). She knew that her role could be more than a mere bubble on the fomenting human sea of chaotic sentiment and fickle pleasure. Should the LORD bless, she could be a link in a chain connecting the past to the future. To Elizabeth, any child would suffice for such a profound charge, yet God entrusted to her a key character in paving the way for the One who would redeem man.

And then Gabriel hails another mother-to-be, Mary: "Greetings, favored one! The LORD is with you...." (Lk 1:28). Why is she favored? Is God favoring her with an out-of-wedlock birth, scandalizing her future husband (Mt 1:19), and damaging her reputation in her community (Mk 6:3; Jn 8:41)? Gabriel clarifies, "...you will conceive in your womb, and bear a son...He will be great and will be called the Son of the Most High... and His kingdom will have no end" (Lk 1:31-33). Gabriel doesn't bother to mention how people will perceive her in the short term; it is enough that generations will look back on her obedience to God with tears of thankfulness. Still, in her submission to God as a mother, Mary receives both the contempt of culture and the favor of God. But note, Mary chose to focus on who truly matters: Jesus, her salvation.

When Mary makes a beeline to her pregnant relative after her little chat with Gabriel, Elizabeth proclaims the truth about Mary's situation, "Blessed are you among women, and blessed is the fruit of your womb!" (Lk 1:42). In short, you are not just going to have a baby; you are going to carry the baby Who will offer salvation to all mothers and babies.

Mary rightly praises God, "My soul exalts the LORD... for behold, from this time on all generations will count me blessed for the Mighty One has done great things for me..." (Lk 1:46, 48-49).

Today many women who face an unplanned pregnancy wring their hands and hearts over "my life now." They are tempted to sacrifice the ancient sanctity of motherhood and family on the altar of empty promises filled with fictional equality, freedom from risk, and continuous pleasure. But there is one inescapable truth proving the folly of that pursuit—death. Death demonstrates that pleasure cannot be our ultimate purpose. Death demands a deeper morality.

Mary understood this, declaring, "He has filled the hungry with good things; and sent away the rich empty-handed" (Lk 1:53). Those who replace godly family for feminized notions of freedom, reject rearing godly children for a career, cast off conception for a larger 401k, or constrict their parental prospects fearing cultural pressure, they are the ones who will remain hungry for that which is truly lasting and good. They are the ones who, while rich in the world's favor, will trudge out their twilight despising the barren loneliness, having eaten feminism's rotten fruit from the hollow tree of absolute liberty.

And while a woman considering abortion often finds herself pregnant precisely because her lifestyle reflects this feminized philosophy, God in His irony uses pregnancy to give her a glimpse of a different future, one where there is life in sacrifice, goodness in hardship, and deep fulfillment in pain. So, her soul stirs with a different sort of future than the one insinuated upon her by a heartless and hopeless world, as the seed of lasting meaning germinates in her heart. Pro-life Christians often stand at this crossroads of grace as she walks the dark woods of her life. And as the Son of God's revelation dawns upon her sad soul, she is finally free.

Questions for Reflection

Why is motherhood important to a woman?

_____

_____

_____

_____

_____

Can you recall your own mother's words of generational impact in your life?

_____

_____

_____

_____

_____

How is it ironic that God uses pregnancy to give a woman considering an abortion a glimpse of a redeemed future?

_____

_____

_____

_____

_____

Father God,

Thank you for mothers and the maternal plan of salvation from one generation to the next. Give hope and strength today to women facing unplanned pregnancies. May they see lasting meaning instead of short-term fictional freedom and pleasure. May you use us to deliver grace. May your Son bring ultimate freedom.

Amen.

Devotion 9
Simeon, The Savior Stirring Hope

Simeon of Jerusalem (Luke 2:25a) is not described as a priest or a prophet, though he may have been. Scripture does not give us any details about his age, his family, or his social status. The Holy Spirit describes Simeon not by any fleeting external measure, but by the weight of his character: righteous and devout (Luke 2:25b). He loved God. And from that taproot grew a strong and genuine concern for people. Simeon's soul mirrored God's passion since "the Holy Spirit was upon him" and he was "looking for the consolation of Israel" (Luke 2:25c).

It had been 400 long years of silence since the confrontational prophetic dialogue between God and a rebellious people recorded by Malachi. Now the Holy Spirit speaks again, but quietly to a man's soul, words of solace: "And it had been revealed to him by the Holy Spirit that he would not see death before he had seen the Lord's Christ" (Luke 2:26). A man who loves God is given God's heart for people.

With such souls there is a clarity that is both sad and hopeful, comprehending both sin and salvation. When God shows a man Himself, that light of revelation displays the extent of his own soul's sickness, against which he is powerless. So, that man is left with a choice—to cast himself on the mercy of God or let the sickness devour him. Simeon, touched by the Lord, displays gratitude for his salvation through devotion to God and a life lived righteously with his fellow man. In short, God gave Simeon hope. And because hope is present in a man who has found God, he is able to have hope for others. Hope is the rope that binds together the need for salvation and the certainty of a Savior.

The vision of God carries a man beyond personal self-awareness. God uses that vision to strip away the facade covering the fallen condition of the world around him too. This transparent view of a broken world is cause for sadness. Yet, this sadness does not lead to despair but rather hope extended—a hopeful watching, an active waiting. Hope is the certainty that just as the Lord's saving presence has dawned upon my soul, so too the Bright Morning Star will rise upon a weary world. The consolation of Simeon is the salvation of Israel, and of the world. The comfort of Simeon is that he would be witness to the coming of the Savior.

So when the Holy Spirit led Simeon into the temple at the exact moment (Luke 2:27) when Mary and Joseph were bringing baby Jesus in to present Him to the Lord, he immediately recognized Jesus for who He is and joyfully sang, "For my eyes have seen Your salvation… A light of revelation to the Gentiles, and the glory of Your people Israel" (Luke 2:30, 32).

Everything changes when Jesus comes. The harsh human formula now includes forgiveness. The bankrupt moral ledger balances. The ship of society run aground rises on His coming tide. Our winter soul thaws to the spring of our Savior's love.

So it is that you and I have hope for a mother considering abortion. We have hope for her preborn baby too. For we have been given it and not for ourselves only, but for people in tormented moments just like these. Women are tempted to despair, trying to dodge a crushing blow from the monster of isolation. And the only path she sees is illuminated by the dull red glow emanating from the ravenous jaws of the dragon of death called abortion. But hope calls to her, "There is another way!"

Pro-life Christians manifest hope through pregnancy centers like CompassCare, illuminating the path to a way out for her and her baby. Poor decisions brought her to this dangerous precipice. Yet, it is at these places in a person's journey when the glitter of this world can be stripped of its power to distract us from the truth: our sin is great, yet our Savior is greater.

Pro-life Christians are like Simeon holding out hope to women for whom death is the only solution. And now, you and I can give her vision, pulling back the shroud to grasp that the coming of her own baby can be a sign pointing the way to salvation found only in the Christ child.

Everything changes when Jesus comes.

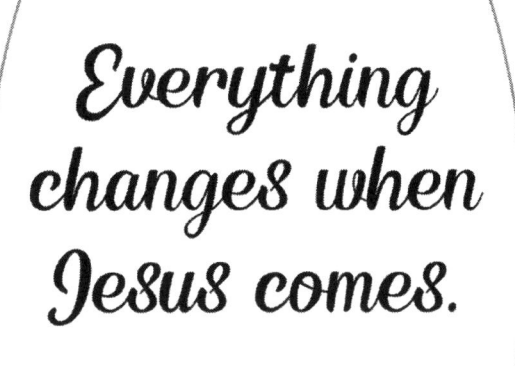

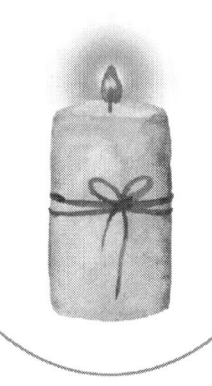

Questions for Reflection

Simeon was a man who loved God and had hope for His people. How might we reflect God's true hope to those around us, specifically to a woman facing an unplanned pregnancy?

_____

_____

_____

_____

_____

What other tangible ways can we offer hope to those whose journey has taken them to a dark place?

_____

_____

_____

_____

_____

How has the truth "our sin is great, yet our Savior is greater" played out in your life?

_____

_____

_____

_____

_____

Father God,

Your word is true. There is great hope found in the Savior of Bethlehem. Teach us to embrace the promises of life found there. And give us the grace and ability to share the hope we have with others. Through the light of Jesus,

Amen.

Devotion 10

Jesus' Plans Lighting the Way to Peace

The birth of Jesus was not a happy coincidence of timing, lineage, and personality so that a little boy with just the right heritage could aspire to be a king over a fledging people. "The record of the genealogy of Jesus the Messiah, the son of David [are]… from the deportation to Babylon to the Messiah, fourteen generations" (Mt. 1:1, 17c). No, Matthew's account reveals that when Jesus came as a baby to Earth, He did not aspire to be a king. He already was the King of all kings, deliberately coming at that time and to that place. Jesus came because all of mankind suffered under the crushing weight of sin as it manifested itself personally and politically.

Our times are not unlike those of Israel's during the days of Ezekiel, deported by sin to the spiritual desert of a materialistic Babylon. Like Israel then, the world today is in desperate need of a Good Shepherd, a Savior King, to lead us out of our sin and out from under the boot of evil leadership, forcing the people ever deeper into the cult of physical well-being. The modern West needs princes and pastors who, like Jesus, seek first to shield the sheep from believing lies, feeding them at great personal cost.

Ezekiel, a prophet during Israel's exile to Babylon, explains that both the leaders and the people were adrift in a void of darkness. Describing the leaders, God says, "Her princes within her are like wolves tearing the prey, by shedding blood and destroying lives in order to get dishonest gain" (Ez. 22:27). We see this in America as her princely politicians push and ram for position by promoting and protecting the slaughter of our sons and daughters through abortion on the idolatrous altar of unfettered personal pleasure. Similarly, "The people of the land have practiced oppression and committed robbery, and they have wronged the poor and needy" (Ez. 22:29a). God through Ezekiel points out that the people's sin was deserving not only their current exile, but His full wrath. What was it they were doing? They "committed adultery with their idols and even caused their sons whom they bore to Me, to pass through the fire to them as food... For when they had slaughtered their children for their idols, they entered My sanctuary on the same day to profane it" (Ez. 23:37b, 39).

Is America's sin of abortion so different? God's view is that when we deem abortion a private matter between a woman and her doctor, or a political matter about which God's people should remain silent, we tacitly participate in the robbery of the neediest of people – preborn boys and girls – thereby betraying our deep spiritual poverty.

Who could save Israel's people from being abused by evil leaders? And who could save Israel from themselves? After all, statesmen are products of the people. So it is that God says, "I searched for a man among them... but I found no one" (Ez. 22:30). Sinful leaders unstop the dam of wickedness which cascades upon society, scattering the sheep, making them food to the flooding lusts of the powerful among them. How do evil leaders behave? "Those who are sickly you have not strengthened, the diseased you have not healed, the broken you have not bound up, the scattered you have not brought back, nor have you sought for the lost; but with force and with severity you have dominated them" (Ez. 34:4).

What is God's solution to the sinful self-exiled and the battered and scattered? Himself. "For thus says the LORD GOD, 'Behold, I Myself will search for my sheep... As a shepherd cares for his herd in the day when he is among his scattered sheep, so I... will deliver them from all the places to which they were scattered on a cloudy and gloomy day" (Ez. 34: 11-12).

We are in the midst of a "cloudy and gloomy day." America's leadership and the behavior of her people exiled us to a moral Babylon. The blind lead the blind. The solution today is the same as it was 2,000 years ago: Immanuel, God with us, the One "to shine upon those who sit in darkness and the shadow of death, to guide our feet into the way of peace" (Luke 1:79). Pro-life Christians through pregnancy centers like CompassCare are doing just that for a woman considering abortion, lighting the way to peace, for her and for her preborn boy or girl.

Questions for Reflection

How is abortion similar to the sin of sacrificing children to idols in the days of Babylon?

___

___

___

___

___

How are the leaders of our culture today leading America along a similar path of destruction?

___

___

___

___

___

What can you do today to offer peace and life to someone around you?

_____

_____

_____

_____

_____

Father God,

Thank you for sending Jesus to be Immanuel, God with us. We pray for the leaders of our country to stand up for life, for hope, and for all things moral and true. Give us the courage to vote and to put these statesmen and women into office. May we embrace the One who came to heal the broken-hearted.

Through Jesus, Amen.

Devotion 11

Wisemen, Heroes, and God's Eternal Kingdom

"Now after Jesus was born in Bethlehem of Judea... magi from the east arrived in Jerusalem, saying, 'Where is He who has been born King of the Jews? For we saw His star in the east and have come to worship Him'" (Mt. 2: 1-2).

Why is the visit from the magi even included in the Gospel account? And why were they so enthusiastic? After all, magi not only represent a pagan occupation, but worship pagan gods. Perhaps the answer lies in the history of their profession. Somehow in their foggy vigilance, they were told of the significance of this King and somehow knew to look for a sign.

Every profession has a hero, be it the pioneer or a pivotal personality within it. The magi would be no different. All theologians have their Luther, all doctors have their Hippocrates, all philosophers have their Aristotle, writers their Shakespeare, engineers their Edison, even ballplayers their Babe Ruth. The mystery of the magi's devotion to Jesus and why it is essential to the gospel may be found in the hero of the magi caste—Daniel.

500 years prior to the magi's arrival in Jerusalem, Daniel saved the lives of everyone in the magi profession. King Nebuchadnezzar decreed to have them all killed for failure to tell him both his dream and its meaning. Finding out about the King's kill order, Daniel convinced the king's guard to wait saying, "Do not destroy the wise men of Babylon" (Dan. 2:24b) until he could tell the king his dream and its meaning. God gave Daniel the ability to do just that, resulting not only in saving the lives of all the wise men, but also in causing the king to install Daniel as "Chief prefect over all the wise men of Babylon" (Dan. 2:48b). Daniel became the champion of the magi.

Everyone ponders the details of their hero's life, the particulars that made him their champion, characteristics to emulate, circumstances to inspire, facts to focus one's own performance. Facts like, how did Daniel find out about the king's dream? And what did the dream mean? This dream, the source of their death sentence, must have become a well of wisdom for these magi. God, through Nebuchadnezzar's dream, revealed the future (Dan. 2:28b). The dream showed the progression of the kingdoms of man through time, all ultimately being destroyed by the Kingdom of God—a stone cut without hands that crushed all other kingdoms (Dan. 2:45a). "In the days of those kings, the God of heaven will set up a kingdom which will never be destroyed... it will crush and put an end to all these kingdoms, but it will itself endure forever" (Dan. 2:44).

Jesus being born of a virgin, "cut out without hands" (Dan. 2:34) is, according to Gabriel's words to Mary, "the Son of the Most High; and the Lord God will give Him the throne of His father David ["born King of the Jews" (Mat. 2:2)]; and His kingdom will have no end" (Lk. 1:32-33). If the magi studied the circumstances of Daniel at all they would have known that the coming of Jesus spelled the end of the rule of man, the dawn of a new era. Jesus is the "Sunrise from on high" (Lk. 1:78b). As Nebuchadnezzar confessed after hearing the interpretation of his dream from Daniel, "Surely your God is... a Lord of kings" (Dan. 2:47). Jesus is King of Kings and Lord of Lords (Rev. 19:16).

"But the stone [Jesus] that struck the statue [kingdoms of man] became a great mountain [the kingdom of God] and filled the whole earth" (Dan. 2:35c). May God's kingdom on earth continue to expand, filling the whole earth, working through His people in places like pro-life pregnancy centers "to shine upon those who sit in darkness and the shadow of death" (Lk. 1:79a). Christmas reminds us of the hope that drives pro-life Christians... that God's rule will win, that injustice like abortion will be done away, that a woman will no longer feel like she must choose between her life or her baby's, that the future is pro-life, and that the light of His kingdom is growing through the sacrifice of His people on behalf of those living in despair and darkness.

When a woman faces the signs of an unplanned pregnancy, her long decision-making journey is driven by thoughts of an unknown child and an uncertain future. But the details of whatever life-road we travel should all end the same as that of the magi, falling to the ground in worship of Jesus as Lord (Mt. 2:11).

Jesus is
King of Kings
and
Lord of
Lords.
Rev 19:16

Questions for Reflection

Who was your childhood hero? What characteristics did they have that inspired you?

_____

_____

_____

_____

_____

How does the vision and ultimate destination of three wise men compare with the magi of Daniel's days?

_____

_____

_____

_____

_____

In light of the magi, how does the baby in the manger bring life and light to dead and dark places?

_____

_____

_____

_____

_____

Father God,

Thank you for sending Jesus to be the King of all kings and the Lord of all lords. Every false idol must fall in His presence. So today, we ask you to defeat the idols of false freedoms, instant gratification, and hedonistic cultural desires. May your truth stand tall and strong in our lives.

Because of Jesus,
Amen.

Devotion 12

Christmas Is an Invasion?

Merry Christmas! "From the days of John the Baptist until now the kingdom of heaven suffers violence, and violent men take it by force" (Mt. 11:12). This is not a verse often quoted during Christmas. One of the reasons is that it is the source of a lot of confusion. Since Christmas is a time to reflect on the coming of the kingdom of heaven in the person of Jesus, describing the effects of His coming is appropriate. The lead-up portrays John the Baptist, from prison, wondering if he should be looking for the Messiah in someone else. Jesus' authoritative teaching and His powerful miracles, juxtaposed with ongoing oppression, did not seem to make a lot of sense to people who believed that Messiah's arrival was going to set Israel free from political subjugation (Mt. 11:1-3). John's question is understandable. Jesus, God in the flesh, and His disciples suffered violence to their reputations, possessions, and persons. Happily, the key verb in this verse could also be translated to read, "From the days of John the Baptist until now the kingdom of heaven advances forcefully, and violent men take it by force." Christmas is a forceful advancement of the kingdom of Heaven. And there is a lot of resistance. Jesus here describes that reality.

Evil never gives up, but God's plan for effecting peace with man is an unstoppable freight train of salvation, proven by God's direct announcement of it to the serpent immediately after the fall of Adam and Eve (Gen. 3:14-15) in the Garden. God then reiterated His salvation plan throughout the law and the prophets (who were killed for saying so). And Jesus, who came for the express purpose of fulfilling the plan, was born under threat of infanticide by the ruler of the day, Herod (Mt. 2:16).

God promised to deliver man from the realm of sin and death and His purposes cannot be thwarted. But while making a way for peace with God, those who refuse to submit to Jesus, wage war. The peace spoken of regarding the coming of Christ is between God and the people who submit to Him. This same advent of peace brings struggle. A few verses earlier Jesus clarifies the strife His disciples should expect saying, "Do not think that I came to bring peace on the earth; I did not come to bring peace, but a sword" (Mt. 10:34). At Christmas, Jesus brings both peace and war.

The birth of Jesus, the Light of the world, was an invasion, a forceful advancement, a premeditated decision to take back what is His, redeeming mankind and the world from the kingdom of death. The coming of John the Baptist overlapping with the birth of Jesus represented the dawn of a new age, the Kingdom of Heaven coming. But violent men will not let go of their power, attacking the King and those who represent Him. There was then, as there continues to be now, much resistance. Jesus said we should expect it, even as John received the message from the Messiah in the darkness of a prison cell, "the blind receive sight... and blessed is he who does not take offense at Me" (Mt. 11:5a, 6).

In the presence of darkness, light can't be anything other than an invasion, the darkness fleeing, shadows bowing.

Jesus is the Light of the World. This metaphor presumes the world is a dark place, "And the darkness did not comprehend it" (Jn. 1:5). Even the father of John the Baptist prophesied about Jesus as "the Sunrise from on high... to shine upon those who sit in darkness and the shadow of death" (Lk. 1:78-79).

Here is the uncomfortable truth: When we step out of the darkness and into the light, we become a target. Too often Christians try to mitigate this reality by hedging and compromising on the truths of what it means to be human under God. But scripture warns against these attempts saying, "You adulteresses, do you not know that friendship with the world is hostility toward God? Therefore, whoever wishes to be a friend of the world makes himself an enemy of God" (Ja. 4:4).

He came to contend, but not with man. His coming represents a full-frontal attack on the reigning kingdom of sin and death. He came to enter into the darkness of death through the cross, dispelling it with the light of His presence. Jesus became sin on our behalf in the sight of God the Father, drank the full cup of the wrath of God's perfect justice upon sin, and the darkness simply could not comprehend Him. So it is that He arose from death victorious, becoming Lord even over the grave! Jesus' self-sacrifice at the cross is a mortal blow to death—violence to end all violence, the hope of resurrection. As the kingdom of Heaven continues advancing forcefully, citizens of His kingdom need not fear the violent men, those that threaten us with our old enemy, death.

Rejoice! For Jesus tells us; "Blessed are those who have been persecuted for the sake of righteous, for theirs is the kingdom of heaven" (Mt. 5:10).

Questions for Reflection

What does it mean that the birth of Jesus was an invasion, a forceful advancement, to take back what was His?

_____

_____

_____

_____

_____

How does this 'violence to end all violence' affect your thoughts about the Christmas season where "peace on earth" is the common greeting?

_____

_____

_____

_____

How do you feel about, and how are you preparing face, the persecution that will come to those who bow their knees to Jesus?

_____

_____

_____

_____

_____

Father God,

Sometimes it's hard to embrace the forceful advancement of your Kingdom in the midst of salutations for 'peace' and 'joy.' Yet, we know that Jesus has come to take back what is rightfully His, us. Thank you! Give us understanding to embrace the joy and life that comes with persecution.

For our joy and your glory!
Amen.

Conclusion

Plumbing the depths of the profound, like the moment when God broke into time and space through the incarnation of Jesus is a privilege. Reflect, marvel, ruminate, wonder. This is the first best response to Christmas. It is what Mary did after angel Gabriel's announcement. It is what John the Baptist did in the womb of Elizabeth when Mary came to stay with her while she was pregnant. It is what the Shepherds did after the choir of angels told them where to find baby Jesus. It is what the wisemen did when they followed the star of Bethlehem and what the widow Anna and devout Simeon did after Mary and Joseph brought the infant child to be dedicated in the Temple.

May our marveling in the salvation of our God be ever new.

About the Author

Rev. James R. Harden, M.Div. is the CEO of CompassCare Pregnancy Services and lives outside of Rochester, NY with his wife and ten children.

Rev. Harden pioneered the first measurable and repeatable medical model in the pregnancy center movement, helping hundreds of centers nationwide become more effective at reaching more women and saving more babies from abortion. He has written extensively on medical ethics, executive leadership, and pro-life strategy. Recently CompassCare's pro-life medical office in Buffalo, NY was firebombed.

Rev. Harden's most recent publication is, _Are You Pro-Life for the Right Reasons?_ He is also the author of the first medical ethics book on women's reproductive health—_Ethical Theory and Pertinent Standards in Women's Reproductive Health_. The book was endorsed by Dr. Edmund D. Pellegrino, M.D., M.A.C.P., Former Chairman of the President's Council on Bioethics, who said, "I commend the work of this commission highly to physicians who seek to practice medicine with integrity in the field of reproductive health."

For more information on how you can save women and babies from abortion, go to CompassCareCommunity.com.

Made in the USA
Middletown, DE
28 September 2024